GEORGE FOREMAN

COOKING $2
ISBN 978-0-9962223
5 2

9 780996 222310

S0-CCZ-857

GEORGE FOREMAN®

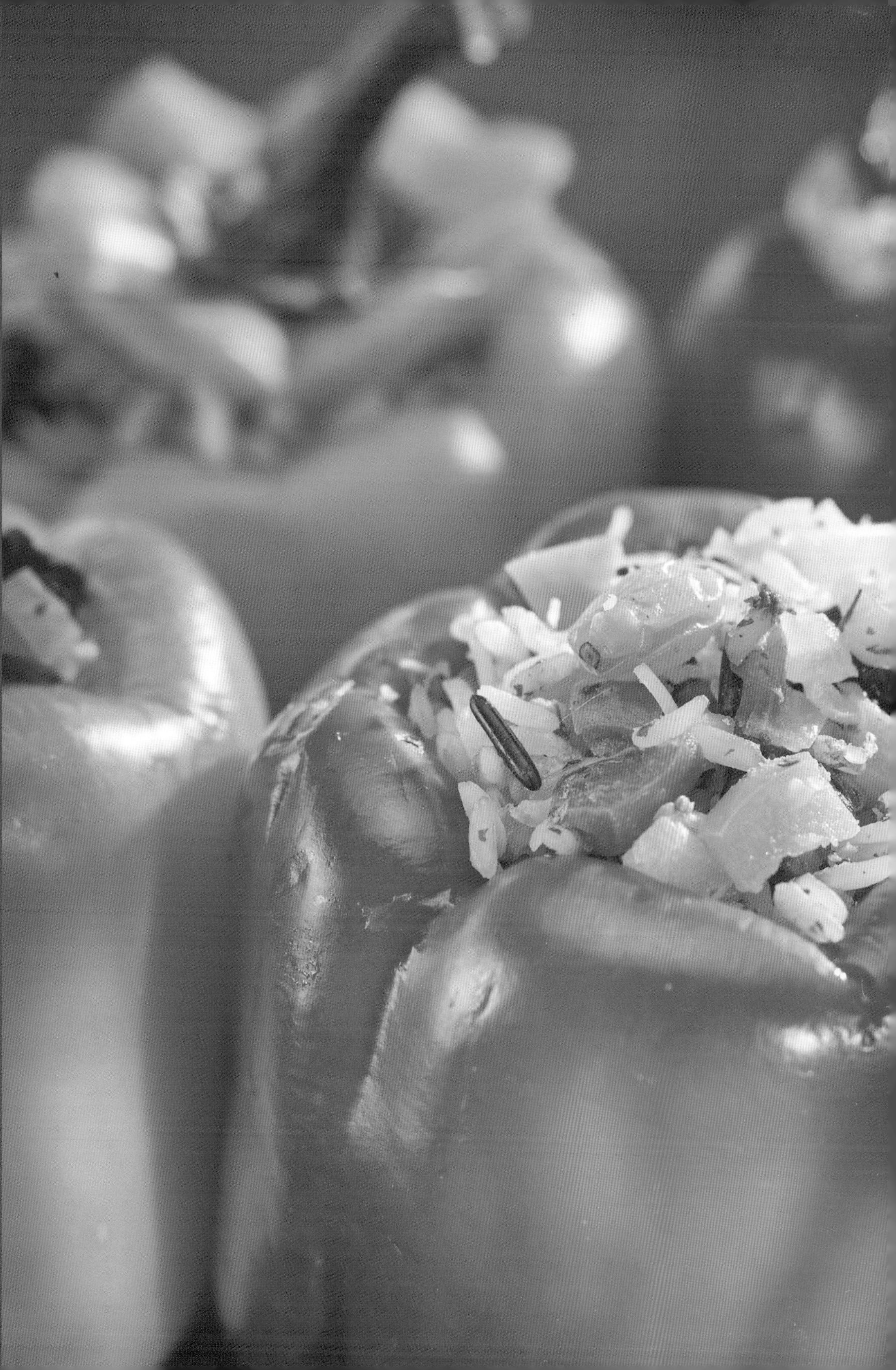

Spectrum
Brands

Published in the United States of America by:

Spectrum Brands, Inc.

Middleton, WI 53562

ISBN: 978-0-9962223-1-0

9 8 7 6 5 4 3 2

GEORGE FOREMAN®

CONTACT
ROASTER
RECIPE BOOK

50 delicious recipes
you'll be amazed with what you can create!

Let's start
Roasting!

A whole roasted chicken, juicy and delicious. A rack of lamb, tender and flavorful. These enticing entrées that would normally require an oversized oven and hours of careful attention are now fast and easy to make thanks to the convenience of the George Foreman® Contact Roaster.

Inside this book you'll discover a medley of recipes for all types of foods: Satisfying main dishes like pot roast or baked mac and cheese; quick and tasty sides like roasted potatoes or classic chicken wings; and even some special dessert recipes for cakes, brownies, and more.

With the all-around heat, a large cooking capacity, and a fat-removing slope, the George Foreman® Contact Roaster makes it easier than ever to create delectable dishes. Try some of the appealing recipes in this book, then improvise your own mouthwatering meals and open up a world of culinary possibilities!

GEORGE FOREMAN®

SIDES & SMALLS

MAIN DISHES

DESSERTS

TABLE OF CONTENTS

sides & small dishes

Create tasty side dishes and tempting appetizers for complete, crowd-pleasing meals. Crab cakes, pot stickers, and chicken wings are just the start to everything you can make in the versatile George Foreman® Contact Roaster. Plus, the all-around heating is great for frozen snacks—the outside breading stays crisp while the inside cooks to perfection!

Roasted Root Veggies – Page 32

Cheesy Vegetable Bake -
Page 28

Bacon Wrapped Apps -
Page 10

Chicken Satay - Page 14

Stuffed Mushrooms -
Page 24

9

30 MINUTES TO THE TABLE IN OR LESS!

BACON
WRAPPED APPS

STACKED TO PERFECTION

Prep Time: 10 minutes ★ Cook Time: 20 minutes ★ 5 servings ★ 2 apps each

INGREDIENTS:

\ 10 slices of raw bacon, cut in half

\ 10 pieces of one (or combination) of the following:

- Large cooked shrimp, peeled and deveined

- Scallops

- Whole water chestnuts

- Pineapple chunks

DIRECTIONS:

\ Wrap bacon around your choice of shrimp, scallops, water chestnuts or pineapple. Secure with toothpicks.

\ Preheat the George Foreman® Contact Roaster.

\ Using tongs, carefully place wrapped appetizers directly in the roaster. Set timer and cook 10 minutes.

\ Turn appetizers over and cook an additional 5 to 10 minutes, or until heated through and bacon is browned.

\ Serve immediately.

30 MINUTES TO THE TABLE IN OR LESS!

BRAT BITES

WITH COLESLAW & GROUND MUSTARD

Prep Time: 10 minutes ★ Cook Time: 10 minutes ★ 12 servings

INGREDIENTS:

\ 3 precooked bratwursts

\ 1 poppy seed bagel, cut into 12 rounds

\ ½ cup coleslaw

\ 12 grape tomatoes

\ 2 Tbsp. stone ground mustard

DIRECTIONS:

\ Preheat the George Foreman® Contact Roaster.

\ Place bratwursts in roaster. Set timer and cook 10 minutes turning over half way through cooking.

\ Remove bratwursts from roaster, cut each into 4 pieces, about one inch in length.

\ To assemble appetizers, spoon 1 tsp. coleslaw on each bagel round. Top with bratwursts, a dab of mustard and grape tomatoes. Secure appetizers with party picks.

Serving Tip:

For full size sandwiches, fill 4 whole bagels with coleslaw, 1/2 of a bratwurst, sliced Roma tomatoes and mustard.

TO THE TABLE IN
30 MINUTES
OR LESS!

CHICKEN SATAY

WITH PEANUT SAUCE

Prep Time: 10 minutes ★ Cook Time: 15 minutes ★ 8 servings ★ 1 skewer each

INGREDIENTS:

CHICKEN SATAY:

\ 1 lb. boneless, skinless chicken thighs

\ ¼ cup ketchup

\ ½ Tbsp. cider vinegar

\ 1 tsp. minced fresh ginger

\ ½ tsp. minced fresh garlic

\ ¼ tsp. chili powder

\ 2 scallions, chopped

PEANUT SAUCE:

\ ½ cup creamy peanut butter

\ 1 can (8 oz.) coconut milk

\ ½ cup agave nectar

\ ½ cup fresh lime juice

\ ¼ cup soy sauce

\ ¼ tsp. red pepper flakes

\ ⅛ tsp. garlic powder

DIRECTIONS:

\ Rinse chicken thighs; pat dry. Cut chicken into strips about 1-inch thick by 3-inches long.

\ Place remaining ingredients with chicken in a large, resealable plastic bag.

\ Thread chicken lengthwise onto 8 (6-inch) skewers.

\ Preheat the George Foreman® Contact Roaster.

\ Place skewers in roaster and cook, covered 5 minutes. Turn skewers and cook 5 minutes more or until chicken is done (160°F).

\ Serve with your favorite peanut sauce.

FOR PEANUT SAUCE:

\ Using food processor or blender, combine all ingredients and mix until a runny sauce is formed

Prepping Tip:
Soak skewers in water before using to prevent charring.

CHICKEN
WINGS

WITH SWEET & TANGY SAUCE

Prep Time: 10 minutes ★ Cook Time: 50 minutes ★ 3 servings ★ 2 wings each

INGREDIENTS:

\ 1 ½ lbs. chicken wings (about 6 wings)

\ Salt and pepper

\ ½ cup sugar

\ ¼ cup grape jelly

\ ¼ cup apple cider vinegar

\ 2 Tbsp. cornstarch

\ 2 Tbsp. soy sauce

\ 1/3 cup water

DIRECTIONS:

\ Prepare chicken wings by breaking the tip of the wing at the joint, then cut tip of wing off using a kitchen shears. Sprinkle wings with salt and pepper to taste.

\ Preheat the George Foreman® Contact Roaster.

\ Place wings in roaster. Cover and cook 15 minutes. Turn wings over and cook 10 minutes more.

\ Mix remaining ingredients in medium microwaveable bowl. Microwave on HIGH 3 to 4 minutes until sauce is heated through.

\ Place wings and sauce into baking pan. Set timer and cook 20 minutes, stirring twice until sauce is thick and translucent.

COLORFUL CORNBREAD

WITH RED & GREEN PEPPERS

Prep Time: 10 minutes ★ Cook Time: 15 minutes ★ 6 servings

INGREDIENTS:

- 1 pkg. (8.5 oz.) corn muffin mix
- 1 cup diced sweet red and green bell pepper

DIRECTIONS:

- Mix corn bread according to package directions. Add peppers, stir to combine.
- Pour batter into the George Foreman® Contact Roaster's lightly greased baking pan.
- Preheat the George Foreman® Contact Roaster.
- Place baking pan into the preheated roaster. Cover and bake 15 minutes.
- Open cover of roaster and let cornbread sit in roaster 10 minutes to set.

CRAB CAKES

WITH AIOLI SAUCE

Prep Time: 5 minutes + 30 minutes for chilling ★ Cook Time: 10 minutes ★ 2 servings

INGREDIENTS:

AIOLI:

¼ cup mayonnaise

1 tsp. minced garlic

1 tsp. lemon juice

½ tsp. yellow mustard

CRAB CAKES:

1 can (6 oz.) white lump crab meat, drained, cartilage removed

1 egg, beaten

1/3 cup bread crumbs

2 Tbsp. mayonnaise

1 Tbsp. Fresh minced parsley

½ tsp. seafood seasoning

Salt and pepper

DIRECTIONS:

\ Mix aioli in small bowl; Cover and refrigerate until ready to use.

\ Combine crab cake ingredients in medium bowl. Cover; refrigerate at least 30 minutes.

\ Form crab cake mixture into four patties.

\ Preheat the George Foreman® Contact Roaster.

\ Place crab cakes in roaster. Cook 10 minutes, turning halfway through cooking until golden brown.

\ Remove crab cakes from roaster and serve with aioli.

21

POT STICKERS

WITH GINGER SAUCE

Prep Time: 5 minutes + 1 hr. for sauce to blend ★ Cook Time: 10 minutes ★ 5-6 servings

INGREDIENTS:

POT STICKERS:

1 pkg. (10-12) Frozen prepared pot stickers, defrosted

1 Tbsp. soy sauce

1 Tbsp. sesame oil

GINGER SAUCE:

1 scallion, finely chopped

¼ cup white wine vinegar

¼ cup soy sauce

1 clove garlic, minced

1 Tbsp. honey

2 tsp. granulated sugar

½ tsp. minced ginger

½ tsp. red pepper flakes

DIRECTIONS:

\ Mix ginger sauce ingredients in a small bowl. Refrigerate at least one hour to allow flavors to blend.

\ Brush pot stickers with soy sauce and sesame oil; set aside.

\ Preheat the George Foreman® Contact Roaster.

\ Place pot stickers in roaster. Set timer and cook 5-10 minutes turning halfway through cooking until heated through and lightly browned.

\ Serve with ginger sauce.

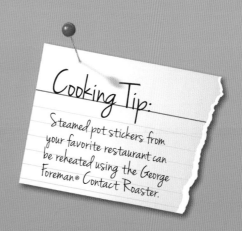

Cooking Tip:

Steamed pot stickers from your favorite restaurant can be reheated using the George Foreman® Contact Roaster.

STUFFED MUSHROOMS

WITH CHEDDAR CHEESE

Prep Time: 5 minutes ★ Cook Time: 10 minutes ★ 6 servings ★ 2 mushrooms each

INGREDIENTS:

\ 12 (1-2 inch diameter) white mushrooms, stems removed

\ ½ cup shredded cheddar cheese

\ ¼ cup chopped green olives

\ ¼ cup black olives, pitted

\ ¼ cup minced red onion

\ 1 garlic clove, minced

\ 1 Tbsp. mayonnaise

DIRECTIONS:

\ To make filling, cut ends off mushroom stems and mince stems.

\ Mix minced mushroom stems with remaining ingredients in small bowl.

\ Spoon 1 tsp. filling into each mushroom cap.

\ Preheat the George Foreman® Contact Roaster.

\ Place filled mushrooms in roaster. Set timer and cook 10 minutes or until mushrooms are heated through.

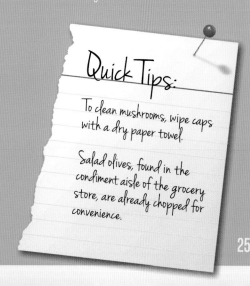

Quick Tips:

To clean mushrooms, wipe caps with a dry paper towel.

Salad olives, found in the condiment aisle of the grocery store, are already chopped for convenience.

25

EGGPLANT
PARMESAN

WITH BASIL PESTO

Prep Time: 5 minutes ★ Cook Time: 30 minutes ★ 2 servings ★ 3 slices each

INGREDIENTS:

1 small eggplant, peeled and sliced into
6 (½-inch) slices

¼ cup Flour

Salt and pepper

1 egg, beaten

½ cup seasoned bread crumbs

1 cup basil pesto sauce

DIRECTIONS:

Using 3 shallow plates, mix flour, salt and pepper in one, egg in the second and bread crumbs in the third.

Dredge each slice of eggplant first in flour, then in egg and lastly in bread crumbs.

Preheat the George Foreman® Contact Roaster.

Brush a little oil in roaster and add eggplant. Set timer and cook covered for 10 minutes or until golden brown. Turn eggplant slices over and cook an additional 10 minutes. Remove from roaster.

Pour basil pesto into baking pan. Set timer; heat 10 minutes. Add eggplant to sauce and serve hot.

30 MINUTES OR LESS! TO THE TABLE IN

CHEESY
VEGETABLE BAKE

TOPPED WITH CRISPY ONION RINGS

Prep Time: 5 minutes ★ Cook Time: 20 minutes ★ 4 servings ★ 1 cup each

INGREDIENTS:

\ 1 Tbsp. butter

\ 1 ½ cup shredded cheddar cheese

\ 1 Tbsp. cornstarch

\ 1 (16 oz.) package frozen cauliflower, broccoli and carrot mix, thawed

\ ½ cup French fried onions

DIRECTIONS:

\ Place butter in baking pan and insert into George Foreman® Contact Roaster. Preheat 5 minutes.

\ Mix cheese and cornstarch together; place in large resealable plastic bag. Add vegetables; mix well.

\ Place vegetable mixture into baking pan. Top evenly with French fried onions.

\ Set timer and bake 15 to 20 minutes or until hot.

TO THE TABLE IN
30 MINUTES
OR LESS!

ROASTED
GARLIC BREAD

WITH BASIL AND GRAPE TOMATOES

Prep Time: 5 minutes ★ Cook Time: 25 minutes ★ 12 servings

INGREDIENTS:

3 large garlic bulbs (about 3-inches in diameter) excess skin removed

1 Tbsp. olive oil

12 slices French bread, buttered and toasted

12 fresh basil leaves

6 grape tomatoes, cut in half

DIRECTIONS:

Preheat the George Foreman® Contact Roaster.

Cut off stem portion of each garlic bulb exposing the garlic cloves. Brush oil on cut side of garlic.

Place garlic bulbs in roaster. Set timer and roast garlic 20 minutes until garlic is just softened. Remove garlic from roaster, cover with foil and set for 10 minutes to cool.

To remove roasted garlic cloves from bulb, squeeze the whole bulb into a small bowl.

Spread garlic on toasted bread, top each toast with basil leaf and one tomato half.

TO THE TABLE IN
30 MINUTES
OR LESS!

ROASTED
ROOT VEGGIES

LIGHTLY SEASONED WITH SALT AND PEPPER

Prep Time: 5 minutes ★ Cook Time: 20 minutes ★ 4 servings

INGREDIENTS:

2 red beets (1 ½ inches in diameter), sliced

2 golden beets (1 ½ inches in diameter), sliced

1 large carrot, cut into 3 inch long, flat pieces

1 large parsnip, cut into 3-inch lengths
and quartered

2 Tbsp. cooking oil

Salt and pepper

DIRECTIONS:

Place cut vegetables, oil, salt and pepper into a large, resealable plastic bag; mix well to coat.

Preheat the George Foreman® Contact Roaster.

Place vegetables flat side down in roaster.

Set timer and roast vegetables for 15 minutes, turning twice until tender, crisp and browned on all sides.

ROASTED
NEW POTATOES

WITH SOUR CREAM SAUCE

Prep Time: 5 minutes ★ Cook Time: 30 minutes ★ 4 servings ★ 1 cup each

INGREDIENTS:

\ ½ cup sour cream

\ 1 (1 oz.) packet dry ranch
(dip & salad dressing) seasoning mix

\ 1 Tbsp. canola oil

\ 1 lb. red skin new potatoes
(1-2 inches in diameter), quartered

DIRECTIONS:

\ Mix sour cream and 1 Tbsp. ranch seasoning mix in small bowl; set aside.

\ Place quartered potatoes and remaining ranch seasoning mix in resealable plastic bag; shake to coat.

\ Insert baking pan in the George Foreman® Contact Roaster; add oil and preheat 5 minutes.

\ Add seasoned potatoes to baking pan. Close lid. Set timer and cook 30 minutes turning potatoes halfway through cooking until potatoes are tender.

\ Serve potatoes with a dollop of seasoned sour cream.

ROASTED
SWEET POTATOES

WITH PEPPER AND CINNAMON

Prep Time: 5 minutes ★ Cook Time: 15 minutes ★ 2 servings

INGREDIENTS:

\ 2 small sweet potatoes cut into rectangular pieces

\ 1 Tbsp. oil

\ 1 tsp. cinnamon

\ 1 tsp. sugar

\ ½ tsp. ground cayenne pepper

DIRECTIONS:

\ Place sweet potatoes, oil and salt and pepper into a large, resealable plastic bag; mix well to coat.

\ Preheat the George Foreman® Contact Roaster.

\ Place potatoes, flat sides down, directly in roaster.

\ Set timer and roast 15 minutes turning twice or until tender, crisp and browned on all sides.

37

ROASTED
VEGETABLES

WITH BALSAMIC VINEGAR

Prep Time: 5 minutes ★ Cook Time: 20 minutes ★ 4 servings

INGREDIENTS:

\ 1 cup baby carrots, cut in half lengthwise

\ 8 baby belle mushrooms, cut in half

\ 1 Tbsp. chopped fresh parsley

\ 1 Tbsp. balsamic vinegar

\ 1 Tbsp. olive oil

\ 1 tsp. coarse ground sea salt

DIRECTIONS:

\ Place all ingredients into a large resealable plastic bag; shake to combine.

\ Preheat the George Foreman® Contact Roaster.

\ Place vegetables in roaster; set timer and cook 20 minutes stirring halfway through cooking. Vegetables should be tender crisp.

Stuffed Peppers - Page 86

Baked Salmon - Page 72

Cornish Hens - Page 58

40

main dishes

Lasagna Roll-Ups - Page 82

Mealtime is under control. Create easy "one-pot" dishes with layers of flavor, or quickly cook meat and seafood for a substantial entrée. The George Foreman® Contact Roaster can take the place of a large roaster, a slow cooker, and a full-size oven. That means you can cook full-size family meals without overheating your kitchen!

42

RIBEYE STEAK

WITH ROASTED CORN

Prep Time: 5 minutes + 15 minutes to marinade ★ Cook Time: 30 minutes ★ 2 servings

INGREDIENTS:

\ 2 small ribeye steaks (about 10 oz.)

\ 1 Tbsp. soy sauce

\ 1 tsp. garlic powder

\ Fresh ground pepper

\ 4 corn on the cob halves

\ 2 Tbsp. vegetable oil

DIRECTIONS:

\ Season steaks with soy sauce, garlic powder and pepper; let marinate 15 minutes.

\ Preheat the George Foreman® Contact Roaster.

\ Brush corn with oil and place in roaster. Set timer and cook covered for 10 minutes.

\ Turn corn, and cook 10 minutes or until corn is done. Remove corn from roaster, cover with foil and set aside.

\ Place marinated steaks in roaster, leave lid open, and cook 10 minutes, turning steak halfway through cooking or until desired doneness is reached.

TO THE TABLE IN
★ ★ ★
30 MINUTES
★ ★ ★
OR LESS!

STUFFED FLANK STEAK

WITH BLUE CHEESE FILLING

Prep Time: 5 minutes ★ Cook Time: 20 minutes ★ 4 servings

INGREDIENTS:

\ 1 lb. flank steak

\ 3/4 cup western salad dressing, divided

\ 1/2 cup blue cheese crumbles

\ 1/2 stick (4 Tbsp.) butter, melted

DIRECTIONS:

\ Marinate steak and ½ cup dressing in a large resealable plastic bag. Let stand at room temperature 1-2 hours turning bag over once during standing time.

\ Remove steak from bag and lay flat on cutting board. Sprinkle blue cheese evenly on top of steak, pressing cheese gently into meat.

\ Roll up steak in a jelly-roll fashion and tie at 2 inch intervals with kitchen twine.

\ Preheat the George Foreman® Contact Roaster.

\ Brush surface of steak with remaining western dressing and place in roaster, seam side down. Set timer and cook 10 minutes.

\ Open lid and carefully turn steak over. Set timer and cook an additional 10 minutes or until desired doneness.

\ Remove steak from roaster. Cover loosely with aluminum foil and allow meat to rest 5-10 minutes before slicing.

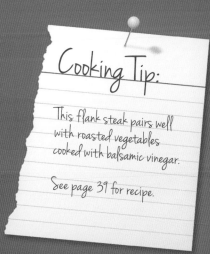

Cooking Tip:

This flank steak pairs well with roasted vegetables cooked with balsamic vinegar.

See page 39 for recipe.

SICILIAN MEAT ROLL

WITH HAM AND CHEESE

Prep Time: 5 minutes ★ Cook Time: 40 minutes ★ 6 servings

INGREDIENTS:

\ 1 egg, slightly beaten

\ ½ cup soft breadcrumbs

\ ¼ cup tomato juice

\ 1 Tbsp. fresh parsley leaves, minced

\ ½ tsp. dried oregano

\ 1 garlic clove, minced

\ 1 lb. lean ground beef

\ 4 slices thinly sliced ham

\ 2/3 cup shredded mozzarella cheese

\ 2 slices mozzarella cheese

DIRECTIONS:

\ Combine first 6 ingredients in medium size bowl.

\ Add ground beef; mix well.

\ Place meat mixture on aluminum foil and pat into a 6 x 12 inch rectangle. Top with sliced ham and shredded cheese.

\ Starting at the short end, roll meat into a log using the foil to lift. Seal edges and ends of meat roll.

\ Preheat the George Foreman® Contact Roaster.

\ Place meat roll seam side down in roaster and set timer for 10 minutes. Close lid; brown 5 minutes. Turn meat over; brown 5 minutes more.

\ Place browned meat in baking pan; set timer to bake 30 minutes or until meat reaches 160°F.

\ Remove pan from roaster; top meat with cheese slices. Let stand 5 minutes before serving.

Tip:
Serve as a main dish or slice and enjoy in a sandwich.

48

CRISPY
ORANGE BEEF

OVER BROWN RICE

Prep Time: 5 minutes + 30 minutes to chill meat ★ Cook Time: 30 minutes ★ 2 servings

INGREDIENTS:

\ 1 lb. thinly sliced beef sirloin steak

\ 4 Tbsp. corn starch

\ 3 Tbsp. soy sauce

\ Peel of 1 orange, sliced into 1x2 inch pieces

\ 3 scallions (cut into 2-inch long pieces)

\ Juice of ½ orange

\ 2 Tbsp. molasses

\ 1 Tbsp. dry sherry

\ 1 Tbsp. rice wine vinegar

\ 1 Tbsp. ginger paste

\ 2 tsp. garlic, minced

\ 1 tsp. sesame oil

\ ½ tsp. red pepper flakes

DIRECTIONS:

\ Slice steaks with grain into 2 to 3-inch wide pieces. Place meat in resealable plastic bag with soy sauce and corn starch. Mix well.

\ Remove meat from bag and place slices in single layer on a wire rack, place rack on cookie sheet. Refrigerate ½ hour until very cold.

\ Preheat the George Foreman® Contact Roaster.

\ Place half of beef, orange peels and scallions in roaster. Set timer and cook 10 minutes. Repeat with remaining beef, orange peels and scallions.

\ Mix remaining ingredients in baking pan. Add meat mixture; stir to combine.

\ Set timer and cook 10 minutes or until hot and sauce is thick and sticks to beef.

\ Serve over brown rice.

Cleaning Tip:

Wipe out roaster using a damp paper towel held with tongs.

49

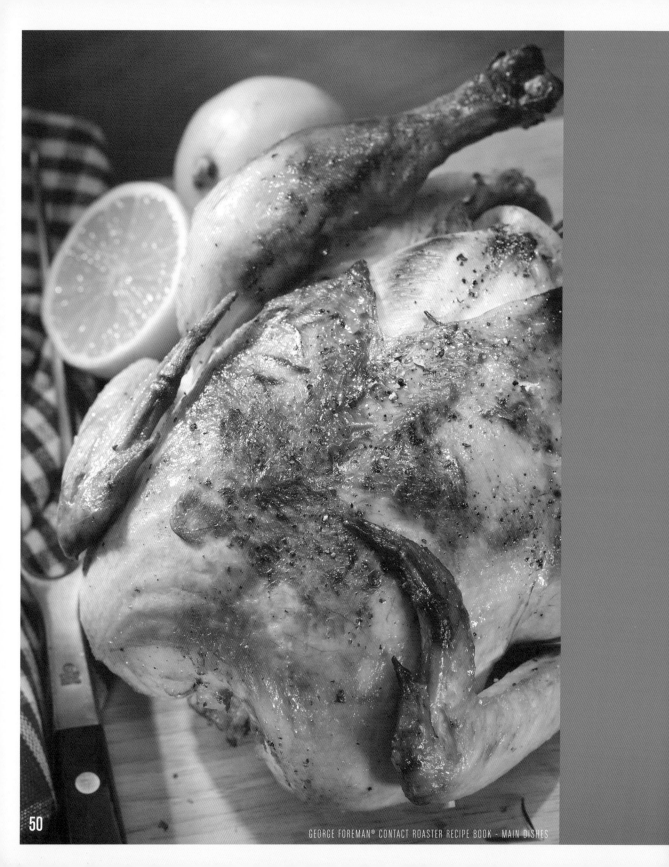

UPSIDE DOWN CHICKEN

ROASTED WITH FRESH HERBS AND LEMON

Prep Time: 10 minutes ★ Cook Time: 60 minutes ★ 4 servings ★ 1-3/4 cups each

INGREDIENTS:

\ 1 (4 lb.) chicken, rinsed and patted dry

\ 2 Tbs. butter, softened

\ ½ Tbsp. fresh minced rosemary

\ ½ Tbsp. fresh minced parsley

\ Salt and pepper to taste

\ 1 lemon cut in half

DIRECTIONS:

\ Preheat the George Foreman® Contact Roaster.

\ Mix butter, parsley and rosemary in small bowl. Rub the butter mixture evenly over the chicken; season with salt and pepper.

\ Cut lemon in half and squeeze the juice of one half lemon over the chicken. Place both lemon halves inside the chicken cavity.

\ Place chicken, breast side down, in roaster. Set timer and roast, covered, 20 minutes.

\ Turn chicken over by inserting sturdy tongs into the cavity and flipping it. Set timer and continue roasting an additional 40 minutes or until done (min. 165°F).

\ Remove chicken from roaster, loosely tent with foil and allow chicken to rest 15 minutes before carving and serving.

30 MINUTES
TO THE TABLE IN
OR LESS!

HERB-CRUSTED CHICKEN BREAST

STUFFED WITH RED & ORANGE BELL PEPPERS

Prep Time: 10 minutes ★ Cook Time: 20 minutes ★ 2 servings

INGREDIENTS:

\ 2 (5 Oz.) boneless, skinless chicken breasts

\ 4 (1/2 inch) red bell pepper strips, cut in half

\ 4 (1/2 inch) orange bell pepper strips, cut in half

\ 1 Tbsp. ground cumin

\ 1 garlic clove, minced

\ 2 Tbsp. fresh parsley, minced

\ 1 Tbsp. olive oil

\ 1 Tbsp. lemon juice

DIRECTIONS:

\ Pat chicken breasts dry with paper towel.

\ Using a paring knife, cut a pocket into the thick end of each breast. Insert pepper strips into the pockets.

\ Mix cumin, garlic and parsley in small bowl. Rub spice mixture onto both sides of the chicken.

\ Preheat the George Foreman® Contact Roaster.

\ Place chicken breasts directly in roaster. Drizzle top of chicken with oil. Set timer, cover and cook 10 minutes.

\ Turn breasts over and cook an additional 5 to 10 minutes or until chicken is cooked (165°F).

\ Squeeze lemon juice over the top of chicken and let stand in covered roaster 5 minutes before serving.

CHICKEN
TIKKA MASALA

WITH SRIRACHA

Prep Time: 5 minutes + 1 hour for marinating ★ Cook Time: 30 minutes ★ 4 servings

INGREDIENTS:

\ 2 boneless skinless chicken breasts cut into 1-inch pieces

\ ¼ cup plain yogurt

\ 1 tsp. Sriracha

\ ½ tsp. ground cumin

\ 2 cups tikka masala sauce

\ 1 cup prepared rice

DIRECTIONS:

\ Place chicken, yogurt, Sriracha sauce and cumin in a 1-gallon resealable plastic bag. Mix and set aside to marinate at least 1 hour.

\ Preheat the George Foreman® Contact Roaster.

\ Carefully place chicken in roaster. Set timer and cook chicken 10 minutes. Turn chicken over and cook an additional 5 minutes or until chicken is done (165°F).

\ Place chicken and masala sauce in the baking pan; set timer and cook 10 to 15 minutes or until hot, stirring halfway through cooking.

\ Serve over cooked rice.

TO THE TABLE IN
30 MINUTES
OR LESS!

CHICKEN ENCHILADAS

WITH CARIBBEAN SEASONINGS

Prep Time: 5 minutes ★ Cook Time: 15 minutes ★ 4 servings

INGREDIENTS:

\ 2 (5 oz.) boneless, skinless chicken breasts

\ 1 Tbsp. Caribbean Jerk seasoning

\ 1 Tbsp. brown sugar

\ 2 Tbsp. cider vinegar

\ 1 Tbsp. olive oil

\ Juice of ½ lime

\ 4 (4-inch) tortillas

\ 1 cup fresh salsa

\ 1 cup Mexican cheese blend

DIRECTIONS:

\ Pat chicken breasts dry with paper towel. Set aside.

\ Combine seasoning, brown sugar and vinegar in small bowl; brush onto both sides of each chicken breast.

\ Preheat the George Foreman® Contact Roaster.

\ Place chicken breast in roaster. Set timer for 10 minutes and cook, turning halfway through cooking or until chicken is browned and cooked through (min. 165°F).

\ Squeeze lime juice over chicken and let rest in roaster 5 minutes.

\ Remove chicken from roaster and cut into ½ inch strips. Divide chicken between the 4 tortillas; roll up enchilada style and place seam-side down in the baking pan.

\ Top enchiladas with cheese and salsa; cook an additional 5 minutes or until salsa is warm and cheese is melted.

CORNISH HENS

HENS

WITH ORANGE GLAZE

Prep Time: 10 minutes ★ Cook Time: 30 minutes ★ 2 servings

INGREDIENTS:

ORANGE GLAZE:

\ 1/4 cup orange marmalade

\ 1 Tbsp. honey

\ 1 tsp. soy sauce

\ 1 tsp. fresh grated ginger

\ 1 tsp. Dijon mustard

CORNISH HENS:

\ 1 Cornish hen cut in half

\ 1 Tbsp. vegetable oil

\ Salt and pepper to taste

DIRECTIONS:

\ Mix glaze ingredients in small bowl; set aside.

\ Preheat the George Foreman® Contact Roaster.

\ Rub hens with oil, sprinkle with salt and pepper.

\ Place hens, breast side down, in roaster. Set timer and roast, covered, 10 minutes to brown.

\ Turn hens over and brush with glaze. Set timer and roast 20 minutes or until done. (min. 165°F). Remove hens from roaster and brush with remaining glaze before serving.

Serving Tip:

Use poultry shears to cut the hen in half. Cut along each side of the back bone and through the breast center. Discard backbone or save it for making stock.

59

ROASTED DUCK

WITH CHERRY BLACKBERRY SAUCE

Prep Time: 5 minutes ★ Cook Time: 25 minutes ★ 2 servings

INGREDIENTS:

\ 1 duck breast (about 7.5 oz.) thawed

\ ½ cup blackberry jelly

\ 1 can (16 oz.) dark sweet cherries, pitted

\ ¼ cup port or sherry wine

\ 1 Tbsp. butter

\ 1 tsp. fresh thyme

DIRECTIONS:

\ Remove any excess fat from duck, leaving skin on. Rinse; pat dry.

\ Using a sharp knife, score skin in both directions. Season with salt and pepper.

\ Microwave jelly, cherries, wine, butter, and thyme in microwavable bowl until butter is melted. Mix until smooth; set aside.

\ Preheat the George Foreman® Contact Roaster.

\ Place duck, skin side down directly in roaster. Spoon 1 Tbsp. cherry juice on breast. Set timer; cook, covered, 5 to 10 minutes to brown.

\ Turn duck over and spoon 1 Tbsp. cherry juice on breast. Set timer; cook, covered 5 to 10 minutes or until duck is cooked (160°F).

\ Remove duck from baking pan, tent with foil and set aside.

\ Place baking pan in roaster, add cherries and remaining juice to pan. Set timer and cook 10 minutes to heat sauce.

\ To serve, slice breast across the grain and serve with sauce.

Shopping Tip:

Duck breast can be found in the freezer section of most grocery stores.

ROASTED
RACK OF LAMB

WITH LEMON-GARLIC SEASONING

Prep Time: 5 minutes ★ Cook Time: 30 minutes ★ 2 servings ★ 3-4 ribs each

INGREDIENTS:

\ 1 (1lb.) rack of lamb
\ Juice of ½ lemon
\ 1 Tbsp. dried rosemary
\ 1 tsp. roasted garlic seasoning
\ 1 tsp. garlic powder

DIRECTIONS:

\ Place lamb and seasonings in a large, resealable plastic bag. Let stand at room temperature 1-2 hours turning bag over to evenly coat meat.

\ Preheat the George Foreman® Contact Roaster.

\ Remove lamb from marinade and place fat and bone side down in roaster. Set timer and cook 10 minutes.

\ Carefully open lid and using hot pads and tongs turn rack of lamb over, set timer and cook 10 minutes. Repeat one more time for a total cook time of 30 minutes.

\ Remove rack of lamb from roaster; place on platter and cover with aluminum foil. Let rest 10 minutes before slicing and serving.

LAMB SHANKS

WITH GARLIC MINT SAUCE

Prep Time: 5 minutes ★ Cook Time: 35 minutes ★ 2 servings ★ 1 shank each

INGREDIENTS:

\ ½ cup mint jelly

\ 1/3 cup lemon juice

\ 1 Tbsp. agave nectar

\ 2 tsp. dry rosemary leaves, crushed

\ 1 tsp. minced garlic

\ 2 (8 oz.) precooked, convenience packaged lamb shanks

DIRECTIONS:

\ Preheat the George Foreman® Contact Roaster.

\ Mix first 5 ingredients; place into baking pan of roaster; mix well. Set timer and cook 5 minutes.

\ Remove pan from roaster and pour sauce into a microwave safe measuring cup. Set aside.

\ Reheat the George Foreman® Contact Roaster 5 minutes with lid closed.

\ Place lamb shanks in roaster, fat side down. Close lid and set timer for 10 minutes.

\ Using hot pads and tongs turn lamb shanks over and brush with 1 Tbsp. mint sauce.

\ Close lid and cook an additional 10 minutes or until heated through.

\ Turn off roaster and let lamb shanks rest in the covered roaster 5 to 10 minutes before serving with remaining sauce.

Cooking Tip:

These lamb shanks pair well with roasted new potatoes seasoned with rosemary, salt and pepper, which can be placed in the roaster with the lamb shanks.

See page 35 for recipe.

STUFFED PORK CHOPS

WITH SPICY PEACH GLAZE

Prep Time: 10 minutes ★ Cook Time: 20 minutes ★ 2 servings

INGREDIENTS:

\ 2 bone in pork chops (about 1-inch thick) trimmed

\ 2 Tbsp. Caribbean Jerk Seasoning

\ ½ cup peach preserves

\ 2 tsp. lemon juice

\ 1 cup prepared cornbread stuffing

DIRECTIONS:

\ Slice each pork chop crosswise in half; fill with cornbread stuffing.

\ Season both sides of pork chops with jerk seasoning, set aside.

\ Preheat the George Foreman® Contact Roaster.

\ Place pork chops in roaster. Set timer and cook 10 minutes with lid closed, to brown.

\ Carefully turn pork chops over and brush browned side of chops with peach preserves. Set timer and cook an additional 10 minutes.

PORK TENDERLOIN

WITH FINGERLING POTATOES

Prep Time: 10 minutes ★ Cook Time: 25 minutes ★ 4 servings

INGREDIENTS:

\ 6 fingerling potatoes

\ 2 lbs. pork tenderloin

\ 2 Tbsp. jalapeño pepper jelly

\ 2 Tbsp. creamy white wine Dijon mustard

DIRECTIONS:

\ Toss potatoes in oil, salt and pepper in a plastic resealable bag. Remove potatoes from bag; set aside. Save the bag for the pork tenderloin.

\ Mix jelly and mustard in small bowl. Place jelly mixture in resealable bag with pork tenderloin. Mix well to coat all sides.

\ Preheat the George Foreman® Contact Roaster.

\ Place tenderloin in roaster, add potatoes. Set timer and cook covered for 10 minutes.

\ Turn tenderloin over and brush with remaining jelly mixture. Cook covered 10 more minutes.

\ Mix jelly and mustard in a small bowl.

\ Remove tenderloin and potatoes from roaster; cover with foil and rest 10 minutes before slicing.

\ Serve with fingerling potatoes.

AUTUMN
PORK LOIN

WITH APPLES & GARLIC

Prep Time: 15 minutes ★ Cook Time: 35 minutes ★ 4 servings

INGREDIENTS:

\ 1 (1 to 1 ½ lb.) pork tenderloin

\ 1 Tbsp. fresh chopped thyme

\ Salt and pepper

\ 4 small baking apples, cored and quartered

\ 1 small, onion, quartered

\ 8 garlic cloves, peeled and crushed

DIRECTIONS:

\ Preheat the George Foreman® Contact Roaster.

\ Rub surface of pork with thyme, salt and pepper.

\ Place pork in roaster. Set timer and cook, covered, 20 minutes turning over halfway through cooking.

\ Add apples, onion and garlic. Cover and cook 15 minutes or until apples and onion are tender and meat is cooked.

BAKED SALMON

WITH CREAMY MUSTARD SAUCE

Prep Time: 5 minutes ★ Cook Time: 20 minutes ★ 4 servings

INGREDIENTS:

\ 2 (1 lb.) salmon fillets, cut into 4 pieces

\ ¼ cup sour cream

\ 2 Tbsp. course ground mustard

\ 2 tsp. lemon juice

\ 1 Tbsp. seafood seasoning

DIRECTIONS:

\ Pat salmon fillets dry with paper towel.

\ Mix sour cream, mustard and lemon juice in small bowl.

\ Spread mixture evenly over each salmon fillet. Sprinkle with seafood seasoning.

\ Preheat the George Foreman® Contact Roaster.

\ Place salmon, skin side down, directly on surface of roaster. Set timer and cook, covered, 10 minutes or until salmon is cooked through (minimum 145°F).

STUFFED TILAPIA

WITH MANGO SALSA

Prep Time: 10 minutes ★ Cook Time: 25 minutes ★ 3 servings

INGREDIENTS:

\ ½ mango, peeled, diced

\ ½ small red onion, diced

\ 2 Tbsp. Pablano pepper, diced

\ 1 Roma tomato, seeded, diced

\ ½ tsp. chili powder

\ 3 tilapia Fillets, thawed

\ Lemon pepper

\ 1 lime, cut in half

DIRECTIONS:

\ Combine mango, onion, pepper and tomato in small bowl. Mix gently; set aside.

\ Season tilapia fillets on both sides with lemon pepper. Spoon ¼ cup mango salsa onto the middle of each fish fillet.

\ Roll up fillets and secure with toothpicks.

\ Preheat the George Foreman® Contact Roaster.

\ Place rolled fillets in roaster. Set timer and cook 10 minutes or until tilapia is white in color.

\ Squeeze lime juice over tilapia before serving.

TUNA SALAD

WITH LEMON THYME VINAIGRETTE

Prep Time: 5 minutes ★ Cook Time: 10 minutes ★ 2 servings

INGREDIENTS:

\ ½ Tbsp. lemon juice

\ 1 tsp. honey Dijon mustard

\ 1 tsp. fresh thyme

\ 2 Tbsp. olive oil for vinaigrette

\ 2 Tbsp. finely diced red onion

\ 1 (8 oz.) tuna steak

\ 1 Tbsp. olive oil for tuna

\ Salt and pepper

\ 2 cups mixed baby greens

DIRECTIONS:

\ Mix lemon juice, mustard, thyme, onion and olive oil in small bowl.
Toss with mixed baby greens.

\ Preheat the George Foreman® Contact Roaster.

\ Brush surface of tuna with oil; sprinkle with salt and pepper.

\ Place tuna in roaster, set timer and cook 5 minutes,
turning halfway through cooking to brown tuna on both sides.

\ Remove tuna from roaster; slice into strips.

\ Place sliced tuna on mixed baby greens and serve.

SHRIMP ETOUFFEE

OVER RICE

Prep Time: 10 minutes ★ Cook Time: 50 minutes ★ 4 servings ★ 1-1/2 cups each

INGREDIENTS:

\ 2 Tbsp. butter

\ 2 Tbsp. flour

\ 1 lb. medium raw shrimp (31 to 40 ct.), peeled and deveined

\ 1 Tbsp. Creole seasoning

\ 1 Tbsp. vegetable oil

\ 1 (14.5 oz.) can diced tomatoes with garlic and onion

\ 1 (14.5 oz.) can fire roasted diced tomatoes

\ 1 Tbsp. dried parsley flakes

\ 1 tsp. hot sauce

\ 1 cup prepared rice

DIRECTIONS:

\ Place butter in baking pan and preheat in George Foreman® Contact Roaster 5 minutes to melt.

\ Add flour and mix with butter using a rubber spatula.

\ Set timer and cook 10 minutes, stirring once or until butter is light brown (roux) and thickened.

\ Stir in tomatoes, parsley and hot sauce.

\ Set timer and cook 15 minutes or until sauce is thickened, stirring occasionally. Remove pan from roaster, set aside on cooling rack.

\ Place shrimp, oil, and Creole seasoning into a medium bowl; toss to coat. Place shrimp in roaster. Set timer and with lid closed, cook 10 minutes or until shrimp are pink in color.

\ Remove shrimp from roaster and mix with sauce in baking pan.

\ Place baking pan in roaster and cook an additional 10 minutes or until hot.

\ Serve with cooked rice and garnish with thinly sliced scallions, if desired.

SHRIMP LINGUINE

WITH CLAM SAUCE

Prep Time: 5 minutes ★ Cook Time: 20 minutes ★ 3 servings

INGREDIENTS:

\ 6 raw, deveined large shrimp, in shell

\ Kosher or coarse salt

\ 2 Tbsp. butter

\ 1 bottle (8 oz.) clam juice

\ ¼ cup white wine

\ 1 packet (1.2 oz.) pesto sauce mix

\ 1 can (15 oz.) fire roasted diced tomatoes

\ 1 tsp. minced garlic

\ ½ pkg. (8 oz.) linguine

DIRECTIONS:

\ Preheat George Foreman® Contact Roaster.

\ Brush shrimp with oil, place in roaster.

\ Set timer and cook 10 minutes, turning halfway through cooking. Remove shrimp from roaster; set aside. Carefully clean bottom of roaster.

\ Place baking pan in roaster, add cooked shrimp (in shell) and remaining ingredients except pasta. Set timer and cook 10-15 minutes or until hot.

\ Meanwhile, cook pasta according to package directions. Drain.

\ Serve shrimp over hot pasta.

82

LASAGNA
ROLL-UPS

WITH ITALIAN SAUSAGE

Prep Time: 15 minutes ★ Cook Time: 35 minutes ★ 6 servings ★ 1 roll each

INGREDIENTS:

\ 1 cup ricotta cheese

\ ½ cup shredded mozzarella cheese

\ 2 Tbsp. grated Parmesan cheese

\ 1 egg

\ ½ lb. bulk Italian sausage, cooked & crumbled

\ 6 lasagna noodles, cooked

\ 1 ½ cups marinara sauce

DIRECTIONS:

\ Mix cheeses, egg and Italian sausage together in a medium bowl.

\ Place about 1/3 cup cheese mixture onto each cooked lasagna noodle; spread to cover edge to edge.

\ Roll up noodles starting with short edge.

\ Place ½ cup marinara sauce in bottom of baking pan. Place rolled lasagna noodles, seam side down, on top of sauce. Cover with remaining sauce.

\ Preheat the George Foreman® Contact Roaster.

\ Place baking pan into roaster and bake 30-35 minutes or until heated through.

MUSHROOM
RAVIOLI BAKE

WITH FRESH BASIL

Prep Time: 5 minutes ★ *Cook Time: 20 minutes* ★ *2 servings*

INGREDIENTS:

\ 1 pkg. (12 oz.) refrigerated mushroom ravioli

\ 2 cups prepared tomato basil soup

\ Fresh basil leaves

DIRECTIONS:

\ Preheat the George Foreman® Contact Roaster.

\ Place ravioli and soup into baking pan; place in roaster.

\ Set timer and cook, covered, 15 to 20 minutes or until soup is heated through.

\ Garnish with basil leaves.

85

86

STUFFED
PEPPERS

WITH WHITE & WILD RICE BLEND

Prep Time: 20 minutes ★ Cook Time: 30 minutes ★ 4 servings

INGREDIENTS:

\ ½ cup raisins

\ ¼ cup apple cider

\ 1 small onion, chopped

\ ½ cup sweet red bell pepper, diced

\ 3 Tbsp. butter

\ ½ tsp. celery salt

\ 1 Tbsp. parsley

\ ½ cup shredded Parmesan cheese

\ 3 cups prepared white and wild rice mix

\ 4 large or 6 small red bell peppers

DIRECTIONS:

\ Soak raisins in apple cider for 15 minutes.

\ Meanwhile, melt butter in large skillet on medium-high heat.

\ Add diced peppers and onion, and sauté for about 5 minutes.

\ Add raisin mixture, celery salt, parsley, and Parmesan cheese to skillet. Continue to cook until cider has evaporated. Remove from heat and stir in prepared rice.

\ Prepare peppers by cutting around the stem to form a lid. Scoop out seeds and ribs and discard. Carefully cut a thin slice off the bottom of peppers so each pepper stands up.

\ Fill each pepper with rice mixture, being careful not to pack rice tightly.

\ Preheat the George Foreman® Contact Roaster.

\ Place filled peppers directly in roaster. Set timer and cook 30 minutes or until peppers are tender.

MAKE-AHEAD
MAC & CHEESE

\\\ NOTE: THIS MUST BE PREPARED AT LEAST 8 HOURS IN ADVANCE

Prep Time: 5 minutes + 8 hrs. to set ★ Cook Time: 30 minutes ★ 6 servings

INGREDIENTS:

\ 4 cups milk

\ 4 cups shredded cheddar cheese

\ 2 cups uncooked elbow macaroni

\ ½ stick (4 Tbsp.) butter, melted

DIRECTIONS:

\ Combine all ingredients in large bowl; mix well.

\ Place macaroni and cheese mixture into baking pan making sure there are no macaroni pieces sticking out of the liquid.

\ Cover pan with plastic wrap; refrigerate 8 hours or overnight.
NOTE: Baking pan will be full - handle carefully to avoid spilling.

\ Preheat the George Foreman® Contact Roaster.

\ Remove baking pan from refrigerator; place into preheated roaster. Set timer and bake 35-45 minutes or until the macaroni and cheese is hot and bubbly.

HEARTY GUMBO

WITH COLORFUL CORNBREAD

Prep Time: 10 minutes ★ Cook Time: 40 minutes ★ 4 servings ★ 1-1/4 cups each

INGREDIENTS:

\ 2 Tbsp. butter

\ 1 small onion, chopped

\ 2 celery stalks, chopped

\ 1 small green bell pepper, chopped

\ 3 garlic cloves, minced

\ 2 Tbsp. flour

\ 2 cups chicken broth

\ 1 (14 ½ oz.) can diced tomatoes

\ 1 cup diced cooked chicken breast

\ 4 oz. kielbasa sausage, sliced

\ 1 cup frozen sliced okra, thawed

\ 2 cups cooked rice

DIRECTIONS:

\ Place butter in baking pan, insert into George Foreman® Contact Roaster. Preheat 5 minutes.

\ Add onion, celery, green pepper and garlic. Set timer and cook 10 minutes, stirring once until vegetables are soft.

\ Stir in flour; set timer and cook 10 minutes to thicken (roux).

\ Stir in chicken broth, tomatoes, chicken, sausage and okra. Set timer and cook 20 to 30 minutes until hot and broth is slightly thickened.

\ Ladle gumbo into bowls and top with rice.

Serving Tip:

This gumbo pairs really well with colorful cornbread.

See page 19 for recipe.

RED BEANS AND RICE

WITH SMOKED SAUSAGE

Prep Time: 5 minutes ★ Cook Time: 30 minutes ★ 4 servings ★ 1-1/2 cups each

INGREDIENTS:

\ 2 cups prepared long grain and wild rice

\ 1 cup pinto beans

\ 1 cup black beans

\ 1 tsp. ground cumin

\ 1 tsp. chili powder

\ ½ tsp. celery salt

\ 1 (8 oz.) smoked sausage, cut into ½ inch slices

\ Hot sauce to taste

DIRECTIONS:

\ Preheat George Foreman® Contact Roaster.

\ Place rice, beans and spices into baking pan; mix well.

\ Place baking pan in roaster, close lid and set timer and cook 15 minutes.

\ Remove baking pan from roaster; set aside.

\ Brown sausage in roaster, about 10 minutes, turning halfway through cooking.

\ Remove sausage from roaster; stir into rice and beans.

\ Return baking pan to roaster and heat 5 minutes more.

SWEET
POTATO SOUP

WITH TURNIPS

Prep Time: 5 minutes ★ Cook Time: 50 minutes ★ 6 servings ★ 1/2 cup each

INGREDIENTS:

\ 1 sweet potato, peeled and cut into ¼-inch rounds

\ 1 turnip, peeled and cut into ¼-inch rounds

\ 3 cloves garlic

\ 1 large shallot, peeled and cut in half

\ 1 Tbsp. vegetable oil

\ 2 cups chicken stock

\ ¼ cup dry wine

\ 1 Tbsp. brown sugar

\ 1 tsp. ground pepper

\ 1 Tbsp. dry parsley flakes

\ ½ tsp. dry thyme

DIRECTIONS:

\ Preheat the George Foreman® Contact Roaster.

\ Place all vegetables and oil in a resealable plastic bag. Mix well.

\ Place vegetables into roaster. Set timer and cook 20 minutes turning vegetables halfway through cooking.

\ Remove vegetables from roaster and place baking pan. Add remaining ingredients and cook covered for 20 minutes or until hot. Cool in covered roaster for 1 hour.

\ Place pan contents into a blender and blend until smooth.

Cooking Tip:
For best results do not fill blender more than 2/3 full.

CHILES RELLENOS

WITH QUESO FRESCO

Prep Time: 5 minutes ★ Cook Time: 30 minutes ★ 3 servings

INGREDIENTS:

\ 3 medium pablano peppers

\ 1 Tbsp. olive oil

\ 3 (1 oz.) Mozzarella cheese sticks

\ 2 cups salsa verde

\ ½ cup (5 oz.) queso fresco cheese

\ ¼ cup chopped cilantro

DIRECTIONS:

\ Preheat the George Foreman® Contact Roaster.

\ Brush oil on whole peppers; place in roaster. Set timer and cook 15 minutes, turning peppers three times to brown all 3 sides.

\ Remove peppers from roaster and place in a paper bag for 15 minutes to soften.

\ Carefully remove skin from peppers.

\ Cut around each stem of pepper to remove seed pocket.

\ Tuck 1 mozzarella stick inside each pepper.

\ Preheat baking pan in George Foreman® Contact Roaster.

\ Place stuffed peppers into baking pan; top with salsa verde. Set timer and cook covered for 10 minutes.

\ Top peppers with queso fresco cheese and cook 5 more minutes or until cheese is melted.

\ Garnish with chopped cilantro.

Cooking Tip:

Placing roasted peppers in a paper bag makes it easier to remove their skins.

97

TO THE TABLE IN
30 MINUTES
OR LESS!

CHILI OMELET

WITH DOUBLE CHEESE

Prep Time: 5 minutes ★ Cook Time: 10 minutes ★ 4 servings

INGREDIENTS:

\ 1 Tbsp. butter

\ 6 eggs

\ ¼ cup milk

\ ½ cup shredded cheddar cheese

\ 4 slices American cheese

\ 1 cup prepared chili

DIRECTIONS:

\ Place butter in baking pan and insert into George Foreman® Contact Roaster. Preheat 5 minutes.

\ Whisk together eggs and milk in medium bowl. Stir in cheese. Pour into preheated baking pan.

\ Set timer and cook covered for 5 minutes.

\ Open lid and using a rubber spatula, gently stir eggs. Cover and cook an additional 5 minutes or until center of eggs are set.

\ Top eggs with cheese and warm chili. Cover and bake 5 minutes.

Cooking Tip:

Use leftovers from homemade chili or your favorite canned chili.

BRUNCH
BAKE

WITH BROCCOLI, HAM & CHEESE

Prep Time: 20 minutes ★ Cook Time: 40 minutes ★ 6 servings

INGREDIENTS:

\ ½ Tbsp. butter

\ 1 cup frozen broccoli florets, defrosted

\ 3 oz. ham, cubed (about 1/3 cup)

\ ¼ cup chopped onion

\ 6 eggs

\ 1 cup milk

\ 1 cup shredded Cheddar cheese,
  2 Tbsp. reserved

\ 1 Tbsp. chopped fresh dill

DIRECTIONS:

\ Beat eggs and milk in medium a bowl until well blended.
  Stir in ham, cheese and dill. Set aside.

\ Place butter in baking pan. Insert pan into the George Foreman®
  Contact Roaster and preheat 5 minutes.

\ Add in broccoli and onion; stir to mix. Set timer and cook covered
  for 10 minutes or until vegetables are tender crisp.

\ Pour egg mixture into baking pan; stir gently.

\ Set timer and bake, covered, 15 minutes. Open cover and fold outer
  edges of egg toward center of pan. Cover and cook 15 minutes
  or until center is set.

\ Remove baking pan from roaster, top with remaining cheese
  and let stand 5 minutes before cutting and serving.

Cooking Tip:

Substitute 1-1/2 cups cholesterol-free egg product for whole eggs or use half whole eggs and half egg whites.

desserts

Complete the deliciousness with a tasty
dessert! The included baking pan makes it
easy to create cakes, cobblers, bread pudding, and
so much more! The George Foreman® Contact Roaster
combines cooking and baking into one convenient package
to give you a great new way to make your favorite sweet treats!

Roasted Apples -
Page 104

Blueberry Buckle -
Page 110

Dark Chocolate Brownies -
Page 116

Pumpkin Bread Pudding -
Page 108

ROASTED APPLES

STUFFED WITH SWEET TOFFEE AND PECANS

Prep Time: 10 minutes ★ Cook Time: 40 minutes ★ 4 servings ★ 1-3/4 cups each

INGREDIENTS:

\ 4 medium size tart apples, cored

\ ¼ cup butter, softened

\ 1 pkg. (5 oz.) hard toffee candies, crushed

\ ¼ cup chopped pecans

\ ¼ cup brown sugar

DIRECTIONS:

\ Cut a small slice from the bottom of each apple so it will stand upright during baking.

\ Mix butter, crushed candies, pecans and brown sugar in a small bowl.

\ Pack the centers of each apple with the toffee filling.

\ Preheat the George Foreman® Contact Roaster.

\ Place apples in roaster. Bake 30 to 40 minutes or until tender crisp.

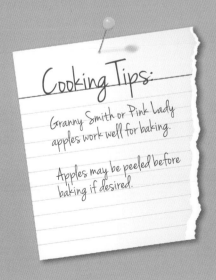

Cooking Tips:

Granny Smith or Pink Lady apples work well for baking.

Apples may be peeled before baking if desired.

ROASTED FRUIT

FOR SALSAS AND DESSERTS

Prep Time: 5 minutes ★ Cook Time: 15 minutes ★ 6 servings

INGREDIENTS:

\ 6 fresh pineapple slices (½-inch thick)

\ 1 nectarine, cut into 6 wedges

\ ¼ cup Sugar

DIRECTIONS:

\ Place all fruit on wire rack, sprinkle sugar over both sides of fruit.

\ Preheat the George Foreman® Contact Roaster.

\ Place fruit in roaster.

\ Set timer and cook, covered, 10 minutes.

\ Using tongs, carefully turn fruit over and cook an additional 5 minutes.

\ Remove fruit from roaster and cool.

PUMPKIN
BREAD PUDDING

WITH APPLES AND PECANS

Prep Time: 10 minutes ★ Cook Time: 45 minutes ★ 6 servings

INGREDIENTS:

\ 6 cups cubed challah bread

\ 1 cup diced tart apples

\ ½ cup pecan halves

\ ¼ cup raisins

\ 2 eggs, beaten

\ ½ cup dark brown sugar plus
  1 Tbsp. reserved for topping

\ 1 cup milk

\ 1 cup canned pumpkin

\ ¼ cup maple syrup

\ 1 tsp. vanilla extract

\ 1 tsp. pumpkin spice

\ ½ tsp. salt

DIRECTIONS:

\ In large mixing bowl; combine bread cubes, apples, pecans and raisins.

\ In medium bowl combine remaining ingredients except 1 Tbsp. brown sugar. Pour egg mixture over bread mixture, mix well and set aside.

\ Insert lightly greased baking pan into George Foreman® Contact Roaster.

\ Preheat the George Foreman® Contact Roaster.

\ Spoon bread pudding into preheated baking pan; set timer and bake covered for 15 minutes.

\ Carefully open lid and gently mix bread pudding. Sprinkle reserved brown sugar evenly on top surface.

\ Bake covered an additional 15 minutes.

\ Unplug roaster and let bread pudding stand covered in roaster 10 minutes to set up.

\ Serve warm with vanilla ice cream or drizzle with half and half.

109

BLUEBERRY BUCKLE

WITH PEACHES AND APPLES

Prep Time: 5 minutes ★ Cook Time: 35 minutes ★ 8 servings ★ 3/4 cups each

INGREDIENTS:

\ 5 Tbsp. butter, softened, divided

\ ¾ cup sugar

\ ¼ cup brown sugar

\ 3 eggs

\ 1 cup flour

\ 1 tsp. baking powder

\ ½ tsp. salt

\ ¼ tsp. ground cinnamon

\ 1 pkg. (16 oz.) frozen peaches, thawed

\ 1 tart apple, cored and diced

\ ½ cup fresh blueberries

\ 2 Tbsp. turbano sugar (sugar in the raw)

\ 1 Tbsp. butter, softened

DIRECTIONS:

\ Cream 4 Tbsp. butter with sugars in a large mixing bowl using an electric hand mixer. Add eggs, one at a time, beating well between each addition. Add flour, baking powder, salt and cinnamon. Fold peaches and apples into the batter; set aside.

\ Preheat the George Foreman® Contact Roaster.

\ Melt remaining 1 Tbsp. butter in baking pan and distribute melted butter evenly on bottom and sides of pan.

\ Spoon batter into baking pan; top evenly with blueberries and turbano sugar. Set timer and bake 15 minutes.

\ Open lid and gently stir the outer batter toward the center of pan. Close lid and bake an additional 15 minutes. Turn off roaster and let stand covered 10 minutes to set.

Serving Tip:
Serve warm with caramel ice cream or cold fresh cream.

PINEAPPLE
UPSIDE DOWN CAKE

Prep Time: 5 minutes ★ Cook Time: 40 minutes ★ 10 servings

INGREDIENTS:

\ 2 Tbsp. butter

\ 1 box (17.4 oz.) Quick Bread and Muffin Mix
with Cinnamon swirl

\ 6 roasted pineapple slices -
(see Roasted Fruit Recipe pg. 107)

\ 7 maraschino cherries

DIRECTIONS:

\ Prepare quick bread according to package directions. Set aside.

\ Preheat the George Foreman® Contact Roaster.

\ Insert baking pan in roaster. Add butter and HALF of the cinnamon
swirl topping from box mix. Cook and stir until butter is melted
and mixture is combined.

\ Spread mixture evenly on bottom of baking pan. Arrange pineapple
slices and maraschino cherries over mixture and partially up the
sides of the baking pan.

\ Top with half batter and remaining cinnamon mixture.

\ Turn roaster off and let cake stand, covered, an additional 10 minutes
to set. Cool cake completely before removing from baking pan.

\ To serve, run a rubber spatula around outside edge of pan to release
cake and invert onto a serving platter.

DESSERTS

LEMON POPPYSEED CAKE
WITH SWEET PLUMS

Prep Time: 10 minutes ★ Cook Time: 40 minutes ★ 10 servings

INGREDIENTS:

\ 1 box (15.6oz.) Lemon Poppyseed Cake Mix
\ 1 ripe red plum, cut into ½-inch pieces

DIRECTIONS:

\ Insert baking pan in George Foreman® Contact Roaster and preheat.
\ Prepare cake mix according to package directions.
\ Lightly grease bottom and sides of baking pan and add batter. Top with plum slices.
\ Set timer and bake covered for 30 minutes.
\ Turn off roaster and allow cake to rest in roaster 10 minutes.

Serving Tip:

Drizzle a thin icing of powdered sugar and milk over the cake before serving.

DARK CHOCOLATE
BROWNIES

WITH BUTTERSCOTCH CHIPS

Prep Time: 5 minutes ★ Cook Time: 40 minutes ★ 12 servings

INGREDIENTS:

\ 1 package (18.4 oz.) dark chocolate brownie mix

\ ½ cup butterscotch chips

DIRECTIONS:

\ Preheat the George Foreman® Contact Roaster.

\ Mix brownies according to package directions. Pour batter into lightly greased baking pan; place into preheated roaster. Set timer and bake covered for 15 minutes.

\ Using a rubber spatula, gently stir batter to distribute outside cooked batter into center of pan.

\ Sprinkle butterscotch chips evenly on top of batter. Close lid and bake an additional 15 minutes. Turn off roaster and let brownies sit in covered roaster 10 minutes to set.

\ Remove baking pan from roaster; cool on wire rack.

\ Cut into pieces to serve.

APPENDIX